BEGINNING UKULELE
FINGERSTYLE
SONG BOOK

UKELIKETHEPROS
© 2020 TERRY CARTER

ISBN-13: 9780982615195
UKELIKETHEPROS.COM
© 2020 TERRY CARTER

TABLE OF CONTENTS

FINGERSTYLE

SONG BOOK

Welcome to the Beginning Ukulele Fingerstyle Songbook for ukulele. This is a perfect songbook for the beginning ukulele player interested in exploring the world of finger style ukulele. I'm excited that you are here, and I cannot wait to for you to get started with playing fingerstyle ukulele. A complete video companion course with step-by-step videos and backing tracks is available by Uke Like The Pros (purchased separately). The goal of the Beginning Ukulele Fingerstyle Songbook is to introduce fingerstyle ukulele playing, and to teach you the finger picking techniques and styles needed for you to move on and play more advanced finger style pieces.

I'm not going to go through various pop songs and show you how to play them, but rather give you the tools and techniques needed to learn on your own to fingerpick any song you want. The Beginning Ukulele Fingerstyle Songbook works well for the beginning fingerstyle ukulele player or the player who is ready to break out of just strumming songs and is ready to challenge themselves

and boost their skill level. This book will also serve as a great warmup for my follow-up book, Ukulele Fingerstyle Mastery, which is also available here on Amazon in both print and Kindle versions.

The Beginning Ukulele Fingerstyle Songbook is a curriculum based, step-by-step book, where each lesson builds your skills one technique at a time. My personal goal is to give you the skills you need to then tackle the pieces in my Ukulele Fingerstyle Mastery book. Because the ukulele is such a great worldwide community-based instrument, I want you to track your progress on the Uke Like The Pros Forum.

Here is what to expect: You will become proficient in 7 of the most commonly used fingerstyle patterns used in ukulele playing. With each fingerstyle pattern, I will introduce 2 separate lessons. The first lesson will be a warm-up exercise where I introduce the finger style pattern and then have you practice it over a very simple 2-chord progression. This way you can focus on learning and memorizing the finger style pattern and not have to worry about switching chords, YET. The second lesson of each finger style pattern will be an original song I wrote just for you, not only to continue to master the finger style pattern, but to have you apply that pattern to different chords so you actually play a song that sounds cool and will make people turn their heads when you are playing it. I will also intermesh the book with different tips and concepts related to finger style ukulele, such as the rest stroke vs. the free stroke.

I wrote the Beginning Ukulele Fingerstyle book on High "G" ukulele, but you can use any soprano, concert, or tenor ukulele with either high "G" or low "G". This is what I need from you.

Make the decision right now that you will stay committed every day until you get through every piece in this book. That means you will set aside some time, even if it's just 15 minutes a day, to practice these exercises and songs. You will only improve and get better with the daily discipline. I realize life it busy with work, families, emergencies, and other unexpected things, but decide right now that no matter what, even if you must get up early or go to bed last, that you will practice. I promise the rewards without outweigh any pain or difficulties you might have to practicing and growing. I'm really excited for you to become a great ukulele finger picker with the Beginning Ukulele Fingerstyle Songbook. Check out Uke Like The Pros for all your ukulele needs. Ready? Let's Go!

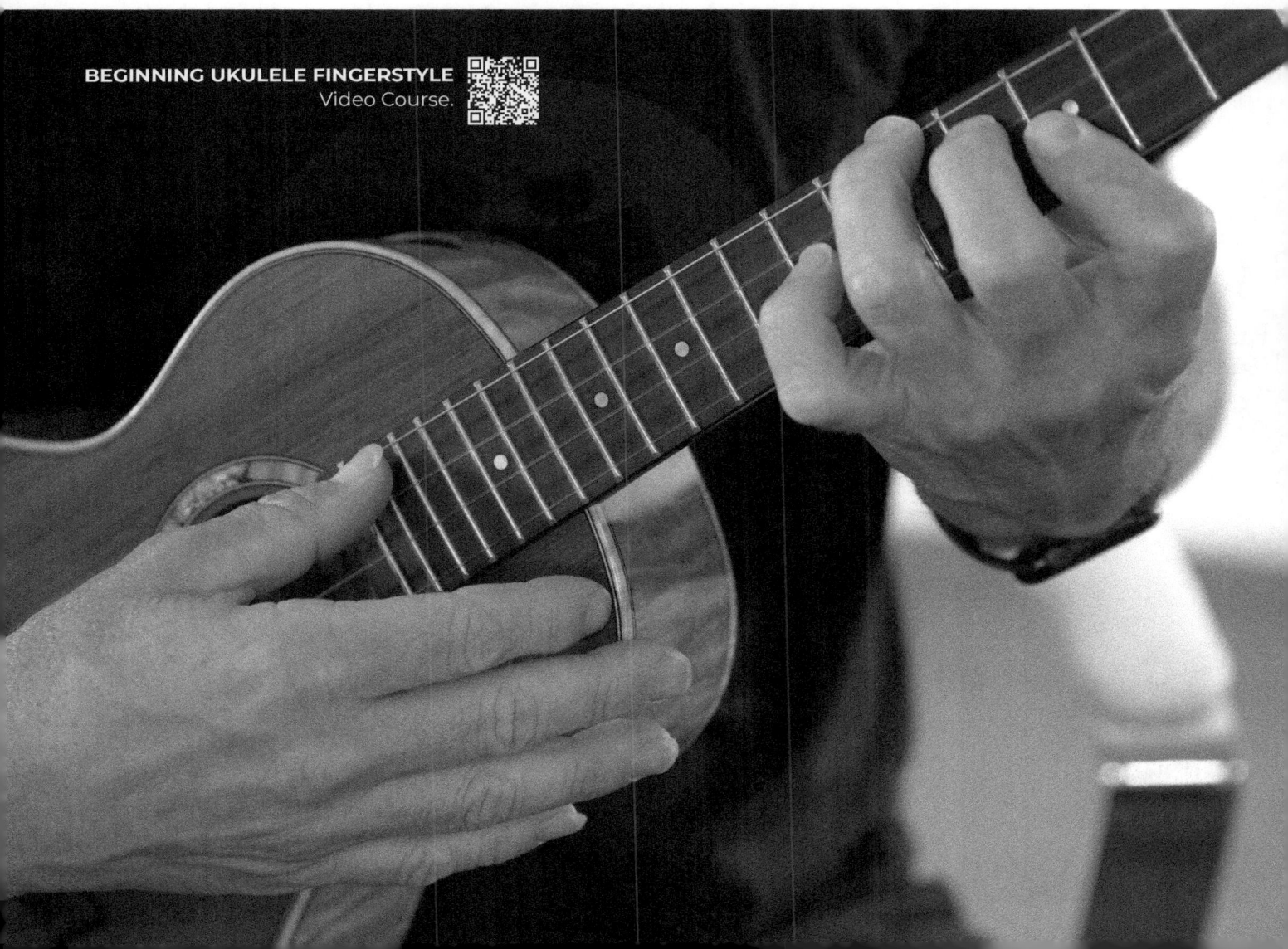

BEGINNING UKULELE FINGERSTYLE
Video Course.

p i PATTERN
LESSON 01

This exercise uses fingerstyle pattern *p- i* (*p*= thumb and *i*= index) which will help prepare for Lesson 02 song, *October Rain*.

by Terry Carter

OCTOBER RAIN
LESSON 02

This song uses alternating *p - i* (p = thumb and i = index) fingerstyle pattern throughout the entire piece. even on the last measure where the thumb will play on the 2nd and 3rd strings.

by Terry Carter

REST & FREE STROKE

LESSON 03

This exerice will help you understand and master the difference between the rest stroke and the free stroke. Each line is repeated twice and the backing track will have 4 clicks before each line starts

by Terry Carter

♩=70

COCONUT'S DREAM
LESSON 04 - *WARMUP*

This piece is a warmup to help you play Coconut's Dream and uses the fingerstyle pattern *p - m - i* (thumb - middle - index). Only use the *p* strum on the last C5 chord. This piece uses triplets which are 3 notes per beat

by Terry Carter

Counting: *1 trip - let   2 trip - let   3 trip - let   4 trip - let*   *Sim...*

Picking Hand: *p   i   m   p   i   m   p   i   m   p   i   m*   *Sim...*

COCONUT'S DREAM

LESSON 05

This song. Coconut's Dream. uses the fingerstyle pattern *p - m - i* (thumb - middle - index) and *p* for the last 2 chords. This piece uses triplets which are 3 notes per beat

by Terry Carter

MERRY-GO-ROUND

LESSON 06 - *WARMUP*

This is a warmup for the Lesson 07 song "Merry-Go-Round." It uses a backward fingerstyle pattern *a m i* (ring, middle, and index) and a triplet (3 notes per beat) rhythm. A backward pattern is when you go from the higher to lower strings.

by Terry Carter

♩=80

C

Counting: 1 trip - let 2 trip - let 3 trip - let 4 trip - let

Picking Hand: a m i a m i a m i a m i

C 7fr.

4 Times

C

1 trip - let 2 trip - let 3 trip - let 4 trip - let

a m i a m i a m i a m i p

MERRY-GO-ROUND
LESSON 07

This song uses a backward fingerstyle pattern ami (ring, middle, and index) and has a triplet feel (3 notes per beat(rhythm. It uses a classic I - vi - IV - V progression (C - Amin - F - G7).

by Terry Carter

CATFISH BLUES

LESSON 08 - *WARMUP*

This song uses the fingerstyle pattern *p - i - m - i* (p = thumb, i = index, m = middle)
on the 3rd, 2nd, and 1st strings. This will be a great warmup for "Catfish Blues."

by Terry Carter

CATFISH BLUES
LESSON 09

This blues song uses the *p - i - m - i* (p = thumb. i = index. m = middle) fingerstyle pattern. Notice it's not a traditional 12 bar blues as it has 13 bars in it. but the ending is awesome.

by Terry Carter

SONNY'S STROLL

LESSON 10 - *WARMUP*

This song in 3/4 time uses the thumb fingerstyle pattern for the entire piece. The biggest challenge is controlling the thumb to only play the strings that each chord requires.

by Terry Carter

JOIN THE UKULELE COMMUNITY
UKELIKETHEPROS.COM

SONNY'S STROLL

This song in 3/4 time uses the fingerstyle pattern *p* (thumb) for the entire piece. Although the chords are all fairly simple. the trick is controlling the thumb to stop on the indicated string.

by Terry Carter

SONNY'S STROLL Pg. 1 of 2

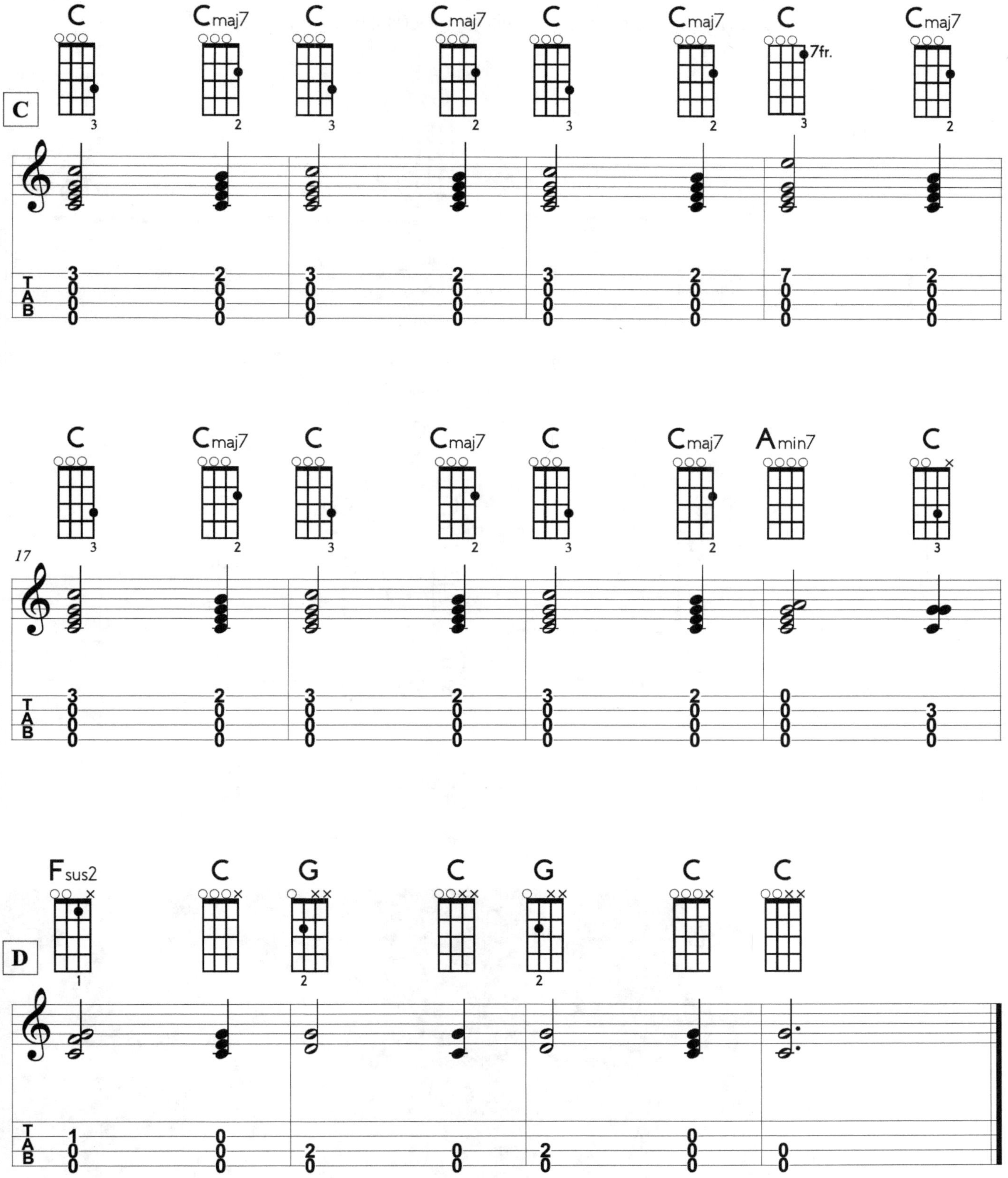

SANDY BEACH
LESSON 12 - *WARMUP*

This song uses the most popular fingerstyle pattern *p i m a* (thumb. index. middle. ring).
This warmup song to 'Sandy Beach' will just focus on the C and the G7 chords.

by Terry Carter

SANDY BEACH
LESSON 13

This song uses the *p - i - m - a* (thumb. index. middle. ring) fingerstyle pattern over the
I - vi - IV - V chord progression in the key of C Major. Notice the very traditional
Hawaiian ukulele ending.

by Terry Carter

CANDLELIGHT
LESSON 14 - *WARMUP*

This song uses the thumb and a 3 finger pinch fingerstyle pattern. It also is in a minor key and uses a drone note (repeating note) on the open 4th string.

by Terry Carter

CANDLELIGHT
LESSON 15

This song is in the key of G Minor and uses the thumb and a 3 finger pinch fingerstyle pattern. It focuses on a drone high G note (low G is fine) and moving chords on strings 1-3.

by Terry Carter

WRITE YOUR OWN PATTERN
LESSON 16

In this challenge you are going to take the C - A7 - D7 - G7 chords and write your own fingerpicking pattern. You can take one of the patterns we did in the challenge or you can write your own. Fill out the TAB and even the notation if you can.

Picking Hand

NEXT
STEPS!

I want to congratulate you for getting through the ULTP Beginning Fingerstyle Ukulele Song Book. I am proud of you for making the commitment to yourself and your playing. You should now have a better understanding of Fingerstyle and its styles, be a more skilled ukulele player, play with better timing, and feel more confident in your abilities.

Now that you are an Ukulele Fingerstyle Master, it's time for you to take the next step in your playing by signing up for a **FREE Month of the Platinum Membership**. Platinum Members have access to over 40 Courses, Challenges, Giveaways, Workshops, and LIVE Q&A sessions with our members.

FREE MONTH

ukelikethepros.com/offer

THE ESSENTIALS

It is important to learn and memorize these terms and symbols because they not only apply to ukulele but to all music.

Treble Clef or "G" Clef

Staff

Time Signature

Measure Numbers

Measure or Bar

Bar Line

End

Top Number:
How Many Beats Per Measure

♩ = 120 — Tempo Marks
120 bpm (beats per minute)

Bottom Number:
What Kind of Note Gets the Beat

Common Time:
Same as 4/4 Time

Repeat Sign

Notes On The Staff: There are seven notes in music (A, B, C, D, E, F, G) and they move up and down alphabetically on the staff.

G A B C D E F G A B C D E F G A B C D E F

How To Remember The Notes:

Notes On The Lines

Notes in The Spaces

E (every)   G (good)   B (boy)   D (does)   F (fine)   F   A   C   E

HOW TO READ TAB

Tablature (TAB) is a form of music reading for ukulele that uses a 4 line staff and numbers. Each line of the staff represents a string on the ukulele and the numbers represent which fret you play on. When looking at the TAB staff it reads like it's upside down on the paper compared to the strings of your ukulele. On the TAB staff, the highest line (closest to the sky) represents the 1st string (A string) of the ukulele, while the lowest line (closest to the ground) represents the 4th string (G string) of the ukulele. When you see 2 or more notes stacked on top of each other on the TAB staff, that means you play those notes at the same time, like a a chord.

UKULELE STRINGS

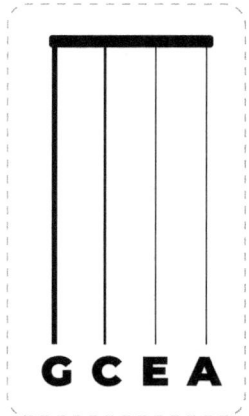

G C E A

1rst STRING EXAMPLES

1) A string. FIRST FRET.
2) A string. THIRD FRET.
3) A string. FIFTH FRET.

2nd STRING - E string. THIRD FRET.

3rd STRING - C string. SECOND FRET.

4th STRING - G string. SIXTH FRET.

CHORD C

ARPEGGIO
USING THE C CHORD

PINCH
USING THE C CHORD

NOTES ON THE UKULELE NECK

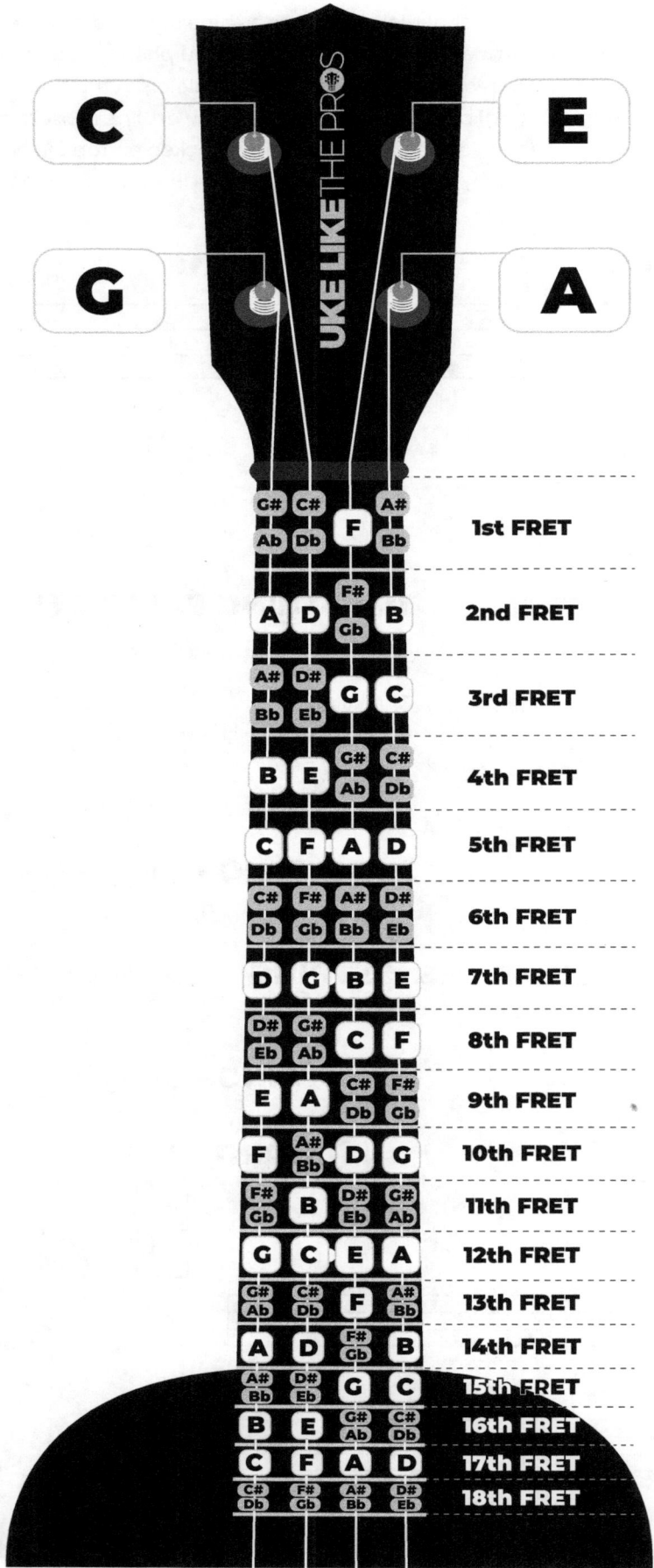

C

E

G

A

UKE LIKE THE PROS

G# / Ab	C# / Db	F	A# / Bb	**1st FRET**
A	D	F# / Gb	B	**2nd FRET**
A# / Bb	D# / Eb	G	C	**3rd FRET**
B	E	G# / Ab	C# / Db	**4th FRET**
C	F	A	D	**5th FRET**
C# / Db	F# / Gb	A# / Bb	D# / Eb	**6th FRET**
D	G	B	E	**7th FRET**
D# / Eb	G# / Ab	C	F	**8th FRET**
E	A	C# / Db	F# / Gb	**9th FRET**
F	A# / Bb	D	G	**10th FRET**
F# / Gb	B	D# / Eb	G# / Ab	**11th FRET**
G	C	E	A	**12th FRET**
G# / Ab	C# / Db	F	A# / Bb	**13th FRET**
A	D	F# / Gb	B	**14th FRET**
A# / Bb	D# / Eb	G	C	**15th FRET**
B	E	G# / Ab	C# / Db	**16th FRET**
C	F	A	D	**17th FRET**
C# / Db	F# / Gb	A# / Bb	D# / Eb	**18th FRET**

C

HEADSTOCK

ULTP SIGNATURE

STRINGS

NUT

FRETS

SIDE DOTS

FRET MARKERS
ON FRETBOARD

SIDE

BODY
FRETBOARD

ROSETTE

SOUND HOLE

TOP

BRIDGE

TUNERS

SADDLE

NECK

BUTT

HEEL

BINDING

SIDE

BACK

MUSIC SYMBOLS TO KNOW

A variety of symbols, articulations, repeats, hammer on's, pull off's, bends, and slides.

Fermata:
Hold note

Staccato:
Play note short

Accent:
Play note loud

Accented Staccato:
Play note
loud + short

Vibrato
Rapid "shaking"
of note

Arpeggiated Chord:
Play the notes in fast
succession from low
to high strings

Grace Note:
Fast embellishment
note played before
the main note

Mute:
"Muffle" sound of
strings either with
left or right hand

Down Stroke:
Pick string(s) with a
downward motion

Up Stroke:
Pick string(s) with
an upward motion

Tie:
Play first note but
do not play second
note that it is tied to

Ledger Lines:
Extend the staff
higher or lower.

Slash Notation:
Repeat notes & rhythms
from previous measure

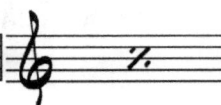

1 Bar Repeat:
Repeat notes &
rhythms from
previous measure

2 Bar Repeat:
Repeat notes & rhythms
from previous 2 measures

Repeat Sign:
(Beginning)

Repeat Sign:
(End)

1st Ending:
Play this part the
first time only

2nd Ending:
Play this part
the second time

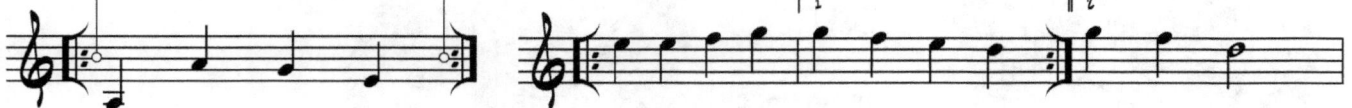

(D.C. AL FINE) — *D.C.* (da capo) means go to the beginning of the tune and stop when you get to *Fine*

(D.C. AL CODA) — *D.C.* means go to the beginning of the tune and jump to *Coda* ⊕ when you see the sign ⊕

(D.S. AL FINE) — *D.S.* (dal segno) means go to the *Sign* 𝄋 and stop when you get to *Fine*

(D.S. AL CODA) — *D.S.* means go to the *Sign* 𝄋 And Jump to the *Coda* ⊕ when you see ⊕

SIM... — Play the same rhythm, strum pattern, or picking pattern as the previous measure

ETC... — Continue the same rhythm, strum pattern, or picking pattern as the previous measure

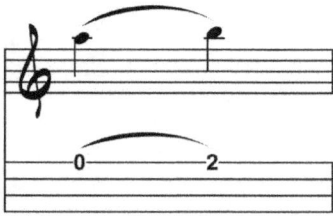

Hammer On:
Pick first note then hammer on
to the next note without picking it.

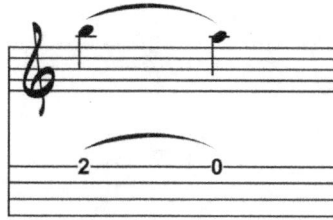

Pull Off:
Pick first note then pull off to
the next note without picking it.

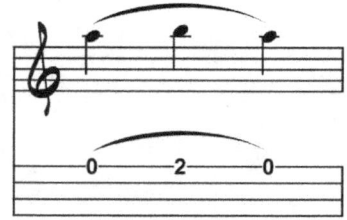

Hammer On & Pull Off:
Pick first note, hammer on to the
next note, and pull off to the last
note all in one motion.

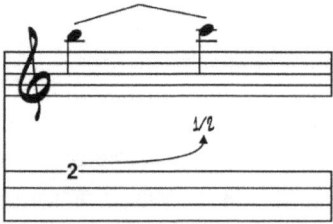

1/2 Step Bend:
Bend the first note
a 1/2 step or 1 fret.

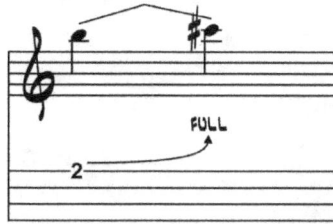

Whole Step Bend:
Bend the first note a whole
step or 2 frets.

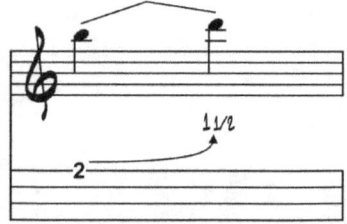

Step & 1/2 Bend:
Bend the first note
1 1/2 steps or 3 frets.

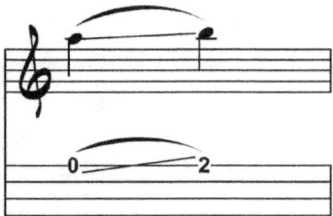

Forward Slide:
Pick first note and slide
up to higher note.

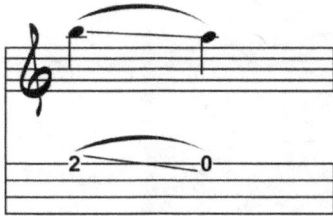

Backward Slide:
Pick first note and
slide back to lower note.

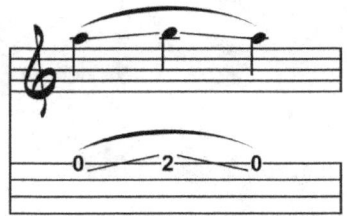

Forward/Backward Slide:
Pick first note, slide up to
next note and then slide back.

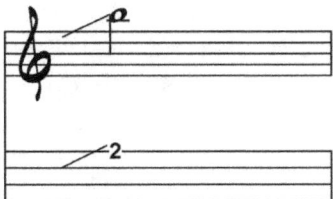

Slide Into Note:
Slide from 2-3 frets below note.

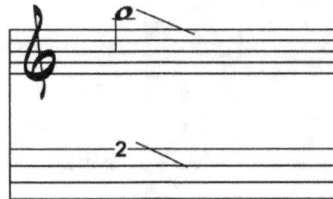

Slide Off Note:
Slide off 2-3 frets after note.

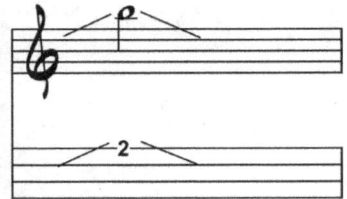

**Slide Into Note
then Slide Off Note.**

F

ABOUT THE AUTHOR

Terry Carter is a San Diego-based ukulele player, surfer, songwriter, and creator of ukelikethepros.com, rocklikethepros.com and terrycartermusicstore.com. With over 25 years as a professional musician, educator and Los Angeles studio musician, Terry has worked with greats like Weezer, Josh Groban, Robby Krieger (The Doors), 2-time Grammy winning composer Christopher Tin (Calling All Dawns), Duff McKagan (Guns N' Roses), Grammy winning producer Charles Goodan (Santana/Rolling Stones), and the Los Angeles Philharmonic. Terry has written and produced tracks for commercials (Discount Tire and Puma) and TV shows, including Scorpion (CBS), Pit Bulls & Parolees (Animal Planet), Trippin', Wildboyz, and The Real World (MTV). He has self-published over 25 books for Uke Like The Pros and Rock Like The Pros, filmed over 30 ukulele and guitar online courses, and has millions of views on his social media channels. Terry received a Master of Music in Studio/Jazz Guitar Performance from University of Southern California and a Bachelor of Music from San Diego State University, with an emphasis in Jazz Studies and Music Education. He has taught at the University of Southern California, San Diego State University, Santa Monica College, Miracosta College, and Los Angeles Trade Tech College.

ONLINE UKULELE COURSES

The perfect place to learn how to play Ukulele, Baritone Ukulele, Guitar and Guitarlele.

ULTP Roadmap
WHERE TO START?

1) UKULELE BEGINNER
A. Beginning Ukulele Starter Course
B. Beginning Ukulele Bootcamp Course
C. Ukulele Fundamentals Course
D. Ukulele Practice & Technique Course
E. Master the Ukulele 1

2) UKULELE INTERMEDIATE
A. Master The Ukulele 2
B. Beginning Music Reading
C. 23 Ultimate Chord Progressions
D. Beginning Ukulele Fingerstyle Course

3) UKULELE ADVANCED
A. Ukulele Blues Mastery Course
B. Beginning Ukulele Soloing Course
C. Fingerstyle Mastery Course
D. Jazz Swing Mastery Course

MORE OPTIONS!

FUNLAND
A. Beginning Ukulele Kids Course Songbook
B. 21 Popular Songs for Ukulele
C. The Best Ukulele Christmas Songs
D. 10 Classic Rock Licks
E. Guitar Fundamentals

BARITONE UKULELE
A. Beginning Baritone Ukulele Bootcamp Course
B. 6 Weeks Baritone Q&A
C. Baritone Blues Mastery Course
D. Beginning Baritone Fingerstyle Course

GUITARLELE
A. Guitarlele Starter Course
B. 6 Weeks Guitarlele Q&A
C. Guitarlele Course for Ukulele and Guitar Players
D. Guitarlele Blues Mastery Course

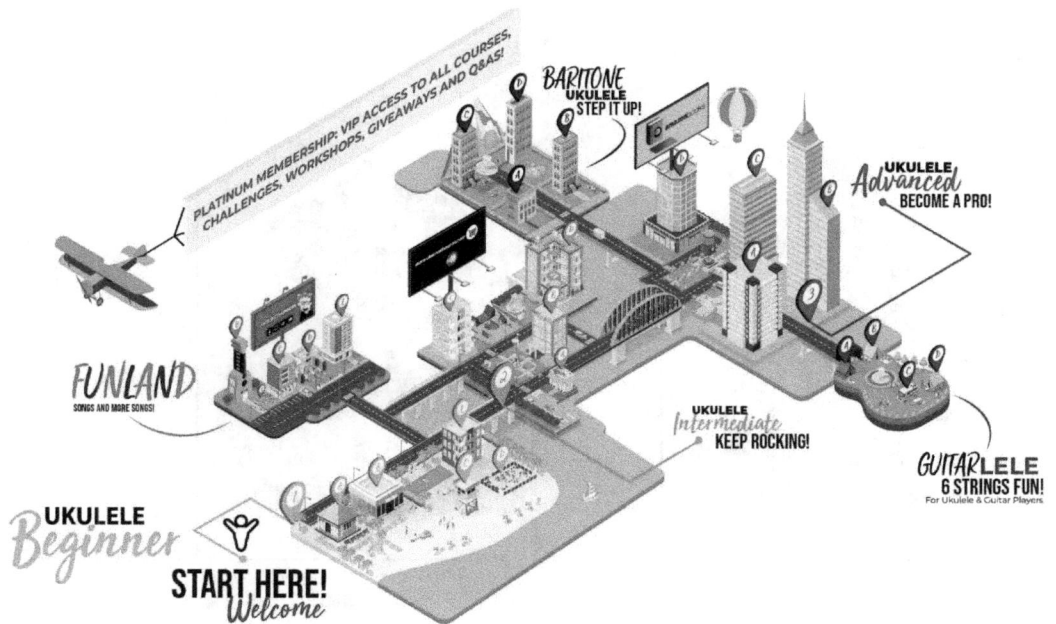

PLATINUM MEMBERSHIP: VIP ACCESS TO ALL COURSES, CHALLENGES, WORKSHOPS, GIVEAWAYS AND Q&AS!

BARITONE UKULELE STEP IT UP!

UKULELE Advanced BECOME A PRO!

UKULELE Intermediate KEEP ROCKING!

GUITARLELE 6 STRINGS FUN!
For Ukulele & Guitar Players

FUNLAND
SONGS AND MORE SONGS!

UKULELE Beginner
START HERE! Welcome

MASTER THE UKULELE #1
UKULELE PRACTICE & TECHNIQUE BOOTCAMP
UKULELE FUNDAMENTALS
BEGINNING UKULELE BOOTCAMP COURSE
BEGINNING UKULELE STARTER COURSE
UKULELE FINGERSTYLE #1

BEGINNING UKULELE MUSIC READING
23 ULTIMATE CHORD PROGRESSIONS
MASTER THE UKULELE #2
UKULELE JAZZ MASTERY #1
BEGINNING UKULELE SOLOING COURSE
UKULELE FINGERSTYLE #2

UKULELE BLUES MASTERY
MASTER THE BARITONE #1
BARITONE FINGERSTYLE #1
BARITONE STRUMMING ESSENTIALS
BARITONE BLUES MASTERY
BEGINNING BARITONE BOOTCAMP COURSE

GUITAR FUNDAMENTALS
UKULELE CHRISTMAS SONGS
21 POPULAR UKULELE SONGS
BEGINNING UKULELE KIDS COURSE
GUITARLELE BLUES MASTERY
GUITARLELE FOR UKULELE & GUITAR PLAYERS

Courses For All Levels
UKELIKETHEPROS.COM

UKELIKETHEPROS.COM
BLOG.UKELIKETHEPROS.COM
TERRYCARTERMUSICSTORE.COM
BUYSTRINGSONLINE.COM

@ukelikethepros

INTERESTED IN **GUITAR CONTENT?**
ROCKLIKETHEPROS.COM

www.ingramcontent.com/pod-product-compliance
Lightning Source LLC
LaVergne TN
LVHW080145090426

835509LV00038BA/1643